Sea Pie

Sea Pie

A Shearsman Anthology
of Oystercatcher Poetry

edited by

Peter Hughes

Shearsman Books

First published in the United Kingdom in 2012 by
Shearsman Books
50 Westons Hill Drive
Emersons Green
BRISTOL
BS16 7DF

Shearsman Books Ltd Registered Office
30–31 St. James Place, Mangotsfield, Bristol BS16 9JB
(this address not for correspondence)

www.shearsman.com

ISBN 978-1-84861-231-0

Introduction and selection copyright © Peter Hughes, 2012.

Copyright in the individual poems presented here remains
with their authors, who have asserted their rights to be identified
as the authors of these works, in accordance with the
Copyrights, Designs and Patents Act of 1988.
All rights reserved.

To the memory of Cliff Hughes
1924–2012

Contents

Introduction	7
John Hall	9
Kelvin Corcoran	11
Emily Critchley	15
Peter Riley	18
Ian Davidson	21
David Rushmer	24
John Welch	27
Maurice Scully	29
Carol Watts	31
Rufo Quintavalle	33
Alistair Noon	35
Lisa Samuels	38
Gerry Loose	40
Allen Fisher	43
Ken Edwards	45
Randolph Healy	46
David Kennedy	48
Alec Finlay	50
Michael Haslam	52
Richard Moorhead	54
Carrie Etter	57
Simon Perril	61
Iain Britton	63
Peter Hughes	66
Anna Mendelssohn	69
Catherine Hales	72
Nathan Thompson	74
Michael Ayres	77
Giles Goodland	80
Sophie Robinson	83
Matina Stamatakis	85

Ralph Hawkins	88
Nigel Wheale	91
Ivano Fermini	94
Rachel Lehrmann	97
Pete Smith	99
Tim Atkins	102
Philip Terry	104
S.J. Fowler	107
Alasdair Paterson	109
Tim Allen	112
Amy Evans	114
Sophie Mayer	116
John James	119
Simon Marsh	121
Further Reading	124

Introduction

In the spirit of the best English poetry of the past, these poets have opted to move on. They make it new without resorting to gimmicks, make it aesthetically potent rather than merely decorative, and make it contemporary rather than modish.

When you are dealing with the very new, as we are here, the merit of individual works of art is bound to be disputed. Some will be ignored, some dismissed, especially by those still relishing the styles of 1956. But, to paraphrase John James, it wasn't like 1956 in 1956 either.

This is a period of political regression, and of the erosion of opportunities for independent thought in education, and of the remoulding of 'consumer tastes' by multinational corporations. In such circumstances it is easy to underestimate the importance of modern art, which begs to differ.

This book displays a series of choices and procedures which are not determined by 'what the market thinks'. These are individual writers investigating and imagining what is true now. They are thinking for themselves, and writing for anyone tired of official versions.

Readers will notice that these writers are different from each other and do not constitute a 'school'. Cultures thrive by means of such diversity, and 'schools' are best reserved for children, fundamentalists and whales.

*   *   *

Oystercatcher Press got off to a good start. The first batch of pamphlets was entered for the inaugural Michael Marks Award and won the publisher's prize. Ian McMillan, Chair of the judges at that time, praised Oystercatcher for 'taking risks with older and newer writers from outside the perceived centre of British poetry'. We must admit that this took place.

Since then many individual pamphlets have been singled out for praise in various quarters. At the same time, attempts to define a 'house style' have generally been thwarted by a new Oystercatcher pamphlet which seemed to be stylistically located on the other side of someone else's fence.

    I think it dangerous for poems or presses to have too clear an idea of where they are going. Just around the corner is a place which is different from where you have been. And it's more fun checking out the locals and locale than grumbling about how this is not the same as yesterday and why are there no chips.

I hope all the people enjoy some of these poems most of the time, whilst keeping on the watch for what's coming up next.

Peter Hughes   *The Old Hunstanton Vortex*

April 2012

John Hall

from The Week's Bad Groan

pale flames of an unruly sun
rise gingerly over the pillow's horizon
from an indented arc

corporately they move me, the shape
they have, to a colourful
love

hollow for a concealed eye, is there
beauty in our lives? does it enter
golden through the hideous (grubby) curtains
to bounce off familiar surfaces, which we angle
do we, in obeisance for the visit

in our dreams we rolled
steadily through the darkened memories
of recent distress, & colourfully rolled
also what we woke to, a world "new" again
in an antique daily wonder

lights driving a clear way through
high banks of grubbily impending
snow

the changeful sleep dropping brightly
in our lives, moving the opening eye
to some remedy

* * *

rise gingerly to the edge
of the week
pale ginger hair caught
in the comb, left by the mirror

the Miró painting of the beautiful
lovers left out of this with the same
regret any fine thing we have found

the admired painting not quite hanging
in my imagination against the rather
grubby lime-green wall
the beautiful lovers left in the mire
of recent distress without their
favourite painter, teaching the young
who offer some corporate resistance & what
is famous about the beautiful lovers is
a certain fragility

Kelvin Corcoran

from What Hit Them

From the hen-roost

'War, one war after another, men start 'em who couldn't put up a good hen-roost.'

1

Black ships drawn up for ten years
to get an exquisite woman, to get at all the women.

To master trade routes, grain supplies, pipelines of wealth
burning lights of acquisition scored on the map.

Make a poem of it; a bayful of weapons in the sun
a poem; the fertile plain a killing ground unrolled

Runs in every direction—delight in slaughter found
the great host fell upon Asia's meadowland and marshes.

2

Karl Twitcher out in the field geologises
no water or gold found but thought
there might be oil out here, let's talk.

Philby bows to the father of his new nation
lips wet from Zamzam, sets about God's work
the American concession secured.

Osama sits on the banks of the River Gash,
wives safely stowed in Khartoum,
sings—ain't gonna study war no more.

At the crossroads of Nejd the Word rose up
from the Buner Mountains, the King of the West,
farming abandoned to wire the faith.

Osama dreams of smart women, burning towers
of Qutb by the waters of Manhattan
of an old bitch gone in the teeth.

Every grain of sand becomes a gem,
and Lord—Israel's tents do shine so bright,
Aramco on the tribal mat, afloat in the Gulf.

3

We had thought them easy meat
for jackals, leopards, wolves
but now . . . across the moat on high ground
Trojans reaping.

It came down hard on us
what if we pull out, wait off shore?
the rampart breached, Europe stranded
by the ships, politicians at the old business.

They go licking up the paid, fat words
in a greased circuit of ignorance;
gods in bliss in Houston and Riyadh
granted the power of massacre.

My brothers dropped in to the sleep
of bronze, their accents mapping
the poor cities of an indifferent country,
as they leaked into the ground.

4

Breathing long alcohol afternoons he might tell me about the war, thick layers of it. The stories thick as beer and rum breath and I still don't know the truth, the final version. He volunteered himself out of the Free State and poverty to cross the Irish Sea, the gulf of sad song misery, for the spit-shine British Army. Out of what? I don't know.

He was shipped out to India and off to fight in Burma with the forgotten 14th. He went on about the filth, the child prostitutes, just girls waiting in alleyways with men shouting the prices. Bored, they would set traps for kites, tie bread with string and allow the birds to swoop down, swallow the bread and fly off, then yank them out of the sky and kill them.

They were half buried in jungle tracks, tunnels of festering vegetation without names, and the stacked humidity just makes you rot—and then, Jesus, the bloody insects at you, at you, all the time—and on top of that the Jap bastards trying to fucking shoot you for free.

And if men like him had not gone to it?

I don't know what they made of their fear; dark bird hovering there for years, just out of vision, ready to slide off the air, dive and tear and shred; one of Chadwick's beasts would do, sharp eyed, clawed. Armitage could identify the model; outline its shape, as it ghosts in and out of the mind for decades.

5

And Thatcher's nasty little war
and Blair's nasty rented wars,
at some point they believe
then retire to revelation on the Red Sea.

We hear their voices like ghosts on the air,
the false tone burning, smeared on a nation.

May their houses be drowned in black dust.
May their words be as waves of dead locusts.
May their fake empire be struck dumb.
And may the names of the dead be made real to them.

6

The bay empties itself, the deep-sea ships sail away
Homer doesn't cover this, if he did I would rewrite it.

The boy looked out to sea, it was empty, he was astonished
—nothing on the radar, just static, just radiation ghosts.

Peace like a white vision, bees murmur in the marram,
and light paints the surface of the whole world.

Somewhere, ships low on the water, take cover,
their discrete weaponry a design feature.

Somewhere, rewritten—speedboats take a punt at the Cole,
Odysseus already dreams of Ithaka pitching under his feet.

And the elemental gods flatten the rampart
as if nothing ever happened here.

Emily Critchley

from Who handles one over the backlash

Waiting

to force these intensities to a shape, to burst
or dilate. Body without cause, so detailed, so collate
and threaded, you find yourself together making verbal patterns,

visual attachments, which you can't unless willing
an escape. If you compere, all concepts can be made concrete,
released suddenly, a movement in commonplace, maybe over

your head. Like I've been searching suddenly all over
for justification. Dicing through bends in the time.
It's suddenly a wall of laughter—warping occasion

on a determined fault line. Or, we are all attached
anyway. Not the same as attack. Bent on understanding,
see? It will curve us as we lean it out. The response

which was so automated, so confused, is more like
keeping up chance, smirched now in the
temperature of the room. High order, it was heady

lately. You had to be there to experience. And even though
one left early, odd throbbing away, ready to hatch.
And though you lay your ear very close to the side of it,

which side have you taken? Responsive or servile?
Others' needs don't curb in the place used to blast
others' intentions for. Can it be generous while qualifying

embrace? The area is warm where thought pounds on it,
day after day, bending pale green shade afterwards.
That's unclear. Or maybe the eye which makes light of or sense anyway
↓
↓
↓

Road Accident

Who handles one over
thegap & thecrash?

      When it's all over,
        cut from it & grab wilting over
some warm desire: metal: the wish of it.
Trailed salt cuticle draped
from an edging.   Nobody's inched perfectly along.

Behind thepowerfulwreck,
just your soft outline bruised
      hedged-in
      dripped formatting.
      Not least before.

      But that was a shame
      not to will it goodbye.

                    Well more
important wait on
at the ploughed skyline.   Eyes up
—reddened on both sides for the ride.

Could've told one as good as new.
Could've stuck to thesideline.
Like reliefs—
marbled in signia: little swan's nests on 1000 or so mini oceans.

    Out there where
        a drunk's
    faltering & spitting,
        1 time out of 10
will there actually *do* something.

Others, smell it, thefear.
    Warm engines   pump out
their love of the ether.

        What cry,
    what does it matter gathering hurt to itself?
        Waste drips all over
every one is

    ruined   fields

    , of no fault
    but their own.

Peter Riley

from Best at Night Alone

(after Deguy)
Singing old songs together in the evening
like nomads round the camp fire. The rare
moment when we agree to die
It is Orpheus, it is the soft thing stronger
than stone, stronger than tree or
scattered creatures, the song in its clearing
as one by one we stand and leave
in good order by the law of random numbers.

They have all gone to bed and left me here.
Singing old songs together in the evening.

* * *

Questions in my hair like midges, buzzing and
getting lost among trees and fading to distance.
Mars, Venus, dusk on earthen spring,
the great fruiting vastness beyond these walls
all the people living their lives and I cannot address
less than that, some favour or dream. Only you listen
are my opening eye, piercing the lights.
Venerable honeyed lips, bitter wine.
Earth's glories pass away.

* * *

Darkness is not a human condition
but a condition of the earth, that renders us
isolated and uniquely empowered at

a turning point and if we are quick and careful
before the light returns in the silence when
people sleep because they think there is nothing to see
there we can reverse the world's drift by
a spasm of thought carried across several mountains
like fire in a fennel stalk. And a bluish paleness
from the night horizons.

* * *

Ekelöf in 1932
I shan't sleep tonight.
Forgive me if I write badly.
Forgive me if I write stupidly.
Death was ignored, and sat there
like some hapless employee.

The bands of night enwrap the house
the wind hisses on the gables
the circular graveyard
turns slowly in the night.
If I am wrong, forgive me.

Memory of a plume of thought
brushing down the hillside like snow
announcing the human victory
and purpose bursts out of enclave.
He got up and opened the window.

* * *

All I ever wanted, a hand touches a wooden table.
And there is nothing to pay, looking at the hills
Through the window and hearing a faint cry from
The cradle, remembering a carved stone at Southwell

Of intricately entwined leafage: somebody was capable
Of setting aside the world's catalogue of ills
And I wanted a lot more than that, a cat's dream
In a quiet basket, of the great fix, the claw in harm.

The claw passes through air and retracts
At the delicate stone edge, the world stands,
It stands alone, not knowing what it wants,

An élite or egalitarian structure. Call it home,
Let it settle round us and hope the wild fires don't
Reach it. There's nothing else either to want or own.

* * *

These hearts always at war,
Twenty years day and night.

O Earth you don't listen, you don't understand,
You don't speak when you see me dying.
O Earth you don't protect your children,
You don't lead them home from the killing fields
You just cry and cry.

Damn these years always at war.
Damn the liars who speak of community.

Ian Davidson

from Familiarity Breeds

No Go Areas

With the surface of the word unfolding new connections occur
Previously impossible to imagine from sites of special interest
Where the next body politic will come from throwing themselves
At the exhaust smothering the world in sound from their insane
Silencers and the baroque ornament of LED lights systems
And stick on spoilers. Silver track suits.

That bunch of middle class kids called new labour are little threat
To the established order or the self interest of the self interested.
The revolutionary sixties a parody of itself in the over confident
Long haired children spat upon by hard faced remnants of the
Industrial working class. Maybe the unions did more than we
Thought possible. Maybe stay at home mothers held

Communities together rather than working all hours to get a
roof over their heads in moments of property madness.
Maybe our imaginations cannot contain whatever comes
Next or reveal the language folded into the
Words where beginning and end curl upwards to conceal the
Filling. Maybe what is hidden is never less than and always

Something more. Maybe the sound of revolution is the alloy
Wheels turning and the residual kindness of community.
Better the curled lip of those that never have all the fruit and
Veg they need or mothers fit to cook them than the overstuffed
Vitamin laden smoothies laced with condescension.
Within the nominal optimism of Chavez lies the word Chav.

I hope he will turn out ok and not sell his soul. Wearing sports gear
And smoking is ironic in the ways inside and outside coincide,

Smoke curling around the lungs and feeding the blood ridden
Veins and starving the brain of oxygen its subversive status
Assured by its new found illegality. The future is unimagined
But cancerous, a dark continent shadowing the breathing and

Where the past is an insecure guide who often gets it wrong.
The new revolutionary guard are of both sexes and impossible
To articulate and therefore temporarily safe from assimilation
At least until the video diaries make the news and spell out
A future. They require a disinclination to play any system and lie
Outside common sense in the flickering nature of humanity

Revealed by every shift in position or new relationships formed
Out of a shifting gaze. It is the law of the father the girls and boys
Fiddling with the bodywork of their little hatchbacks and
Challenging any sense of structural integrity and then
Going out to spit on the students or pink tracksuits or
Hair pulled back until tears come or escaping representation.

Beach Head

Below a certain size rock
becomes sand or other
ornamentation. Below a certain
size plastic particles become

indistinguishable from sand.
Breached below the waterline
the shore becomes a container
for anything that might be lost,

a clutch bag for the
ornaments the world
discards, a necklace of rare
plastic objects to adorn its

skin or the dusting of
light that sparkles from
the surface scratched away
through exposure to salt water

and inorganic to the last. A
chair to stare out to sea
and watch the beach slowly
piling up into unidentified

particles of plastic nets and
the debris from the fishing left
as lace to hang from
the shoulder of a cliff

or an arm stuck out
across the sea or spit
of land between your eyes
with no way to disentangle

sand from plastic or
the ornamental. Sand
drifting; in the middle
of the ocean

a plastic lake, the
items rubbing up
against each other small
yellow ducks bobbing.

Things come together
then disintegrate. Things
are full of dread,
the world, in its best dress.

David Rushmer

from Blanchot's Ghost

The Disappeared

        what you did not write has been written
            absorbed   indifferent to
        the possibility
                  to language, behind
nothingness,
it seeks
                  to be found
     redirection, the displacement
        beyond this: null,
  this emptiness inside,   open up
    reflection, with its own gravity
  withdraws
again from nothing
      formed,
  this presence
  :as an interior
           twilight,
     unfold it
  inscribe it in space,
  in his eyes
     the movement which carries him forward,
         Or that opening
morning
           the impossibility
         exists and merges
  the source of his existence
         when it was inside merges
     the outside
           night of possibility
             what bursts
  enclosed in the sentence "

        disappeared, it has become
 a reflection of them.
colliding
   is disappearing.
      secret intimacy
           Another
           living substance
           to merge with him.
someone else's voice,
              pure night
             itself within
       cannot be grasped.
      outside of him,
   absorbed into the workings
      a nothingness
          in the act
    of disappearing.

The Duplicity

        the duplicity of the world
            a beginning
            death is sometimes the work
connected to finitude
    the possibility
    dissolves too
            to go beyond it
the other   as horror
            always remains
                      dissociate where distance holds us
                      remote movement
                      far from ourselves
            intimate passion
            along this transformation
as reflection from the movement
            outside ecstasy
            enters equivocal limit
            any interval
        absorbed its reflection
            draws itself up
        to the universe
        to create itself
        to act on the impossible
a movement to recapture negation
constantly threatening to vanish

John Welch

from Untold Wealth

At night we found a deserted city
Water ran under the streets
The houses dry and full of herbs
                    Roland Penrose

Imagined scattering coins
In a city of future ruins

Enough of it's   to fall   here's scarcely a sound
There's a god sitting in the air

These fragments hustled away
Fall of a leaf   Shallow wealth

Screen-flicker   translates into riches
Hidden carefully behind trees.

And here's a coin spun in the air   brief shine
Its lyric gleam

But being entirely without substance
The trick of it's keeping the thing in the air

Like the scribble of smoke from a sacrifice
Finding its way to the sky

Here   flights of capital   pigeons
They're turning turning on a depthless sky

The new city borderless
Its city gates become a set of shadows

It's an empire built out of signs
A place of odd meaningless arenas

'Palladiums are where it rightly lives'
Its empty lyric performance

Electrum gleam in river sand
King with a mouth of gold

A ritual to open the statue's mouth
Put back the tongue and a sturdy measure?

To circle the metal's rough substance—
Dead legend. Missing it now

Although I was bathed in its light
And a stadium whispered its crowds

I who went out walking
As if I had scarcely begun

Maurice Scully

from Work

Self Portrait as Oddity

Good when a branch scrapes the roof of your shed
in the wind at night, tapping and telling, saying
good, good to be alive, good to hear, tell, remember,
project, good just to sit down and listen in the dark.

Tear it up and start again.

Knurled brass god-monster, allegoric figure of persistent stress,
grins through fissure in roof at Struggling Writer at Desk. Pale
moon-print shock. Go Struggle, Boy! Thus Hope, done as a
laughing statue & set on a green dome in high, bright light, over
the majestic gates to the city, cameras affixed, each fidget, each
shadow, each crimp in the world-sheet, each suppressed wail of
their cars on the trail policed; granite. And that's that.

.

Then suddenly … Suddenly yr birth-date prints—moist to
paper—lips together after some tart quip—ink on a turning
roll—its dash narrowing, arrowing forward, forward to yr
death-date, then stopped before a little white space, glistening—
that other—the melodrama of this secret printing …

Tear it up, and start again.

What gouges your wax today, what light falls on which
encrustations of ego-shell now? Good question. Thanks. So.
Turn this monument around, have a good look. The Department
of Special Pleading still thrives, I see. And the Hidden Department
of Constant Money-Worry.

Good.

Climb the stairs to the light. Off this landing
many sub-Departments of Ratified Aesthetic Delight.
Language, the Tangible World. Art.

Jurisprudence.

Further up we have a little pool of Philosophy
(greatly depleted over the last decade, I'm afraid)
and at the top, living tip of this Curiosity, is its
        Turbine of Incessant, Coherent Note-Taking.

Splashes. Sparks.

.

> *A child-bed on a narrow landing*
> *by a deep-set window on the dark.*
> *My uncles in the next room discussing tomorrow's*
> *weather in bed. It is fifty years ago. On a farm.*
>
> *I am five. Snails move over an old pan outside.*
> *The yard is black. A tree shifts. Everybody is*
> *dead now, except this voice here talking to you,*
> *to you, to this, to let you know a sort of happiness,*
> *despite everything, yes—a yellow claw descends,*
> *a hen clucks & blinks—a kind of human mist*
> *is drifting across from that place somehow*
> *to here. I hear it. Feel-hear it. Here it is.*

Good.

Good when a branch scrapes a roof in wind at night
tapping and telling, humming *good—good to be alive,*
good to hear, tell, remember, project, good just to
sit down and listen in the dark.

Carol Watts

from where blue light falls 2

11

see so many fly
are buoyant

odysseys   franchised by
breathless   curvature

beyond beam-ends   step
off after   magnetic   nocturnal

orientation   see limits
ever in contention   peeling away

the globe   a bitter sac
tested for risk

in jet hypodermics   the pain
each waking hour   of

falling   let's suppose
you step out in to the air

13

where they sleep on the wing
accumulating

small stones   at highest
altitude   meeting daily ascension

feathered belt of meteors
gizzards   slow beat

in search of   years   suspended
undisturbed by dreams

suppose you find this   distribution
what cups it   and you

spinning   towards night
continuously

or by day

Rufo Quintavalle

from Make Nothing Happen

Letter from Iceland

I. Earthquake

Peace, the sun, a whimbrel on the grass
and under this the thing that nags
and shakes the house, and makes you write:
Peace, the sun, a whimbrel.

II. Hot tub

I'm sitting in the hot tub in the rain and the rain
is coming down sideways
so my chest and face are getting cold
while my fundament heats from underneath
like
one
of
those
long
thin
things
in
deep
sea
vents
that mine a difference in heat for life;
it seems that that there is and not that there is not
is down, in no small part, to them
so I open a beer and sit in the hot tub in the rain.

III. Keldur

I don't understand anything: why I came into
    this body, this life;
my wife says I think too much,
    that I have too much free time,
but I wouldn't want less, and besides,
    I'd hardly call it free.
Up the road there is what was a house
    and now is a building on a farm;
before the house there was nothing,
    and around the farm there is nothing still.

IV. The monks

Like sperm come too late to an egg the monks
arrived in their coracles, wriggled, prayed
on the coast a while, then passed; they left no trace.

V. Sanctity

You put out to sea and nine times in ten
it's suicide; otherwise sanctity.

Alistair Noon

from At the Emptying of Dustbins

1

The snow-clearing begins
with shovels' percussion on pavements.
The Gosplans are finished, new Urals will rise
from spades and brooms. The stations

remain crested with letters from the Greeks,
begotten from the Phoenicians, and Pharaoh's scribe:
GLORY TO THE POWER OF THE SOVIETS. Iron pipes
boil to a seven-month plan, and seasons

will separate at the iron door.
The Old Believers are dead, or deluded
in trams and trolleybuses, on boulevards.
Above tower blocks, no cranes wave arms.

2

Cromwell-shamed peasants are sulking in line.
Will the bread run out? The baker stocks
a lorry-load of Snickers, the slick new font.
Eve's on the till, white-coated, black-eyed.

Give us something to down our Stolichnaya with.
The white clouds rain down crumbs.

3

This is the City of Crows,
as far from Kremlin walls
as from Black Sea beaches,
where seven-month snows
bed down to the calls
of cold birds, their repeated speeches.

This is the turn in the game—
queens gone, king on the run—
where the initiative switches.
Time to retrain and rename,
make moves towards the shifting sun,
reposition an empire's riches.

4

The tanks crawl back to barracks,
their crews glum in summer uniforms.
The addicts of numbness are tripping on full tumblers
and still screaming in the Afghan valleys.
Strategists of the sixty-four squares
and experts on seventies rock and blues,
tell jokes, from Lenin to Brezhnev,
about the evermore dissolving cause.
This is the punchline, the unforeseen
end of the definitive.

5

Mikhail the Domestically Detested
and George the Unfortunate Progenitor
have thawed in Iceland. Yugoslavia is at war.

Someone is strumming unplugged,
the chords reeling down a stairwell.
Where's the melancholy, alcoholic nose
of Belkin, with his squirrelish name
and ear for slang and news?

Sudden sunshine, twenty degrees,
and still they wear scarves and fur hats.
The Winter has slushed out
on the Spring-doubting streets.

Lisa Samuels

from Throe

This bus kneels on request

1.
A man spends his life in an airship
following the sun. Sweating in romance duds.
The narrative was the artery: a pair of lips, a pair of eyes.
'You kissed yourself through me. I wasn't there.'

2.
They show their bellies here, small wastrels to the sea
a full of feeling complement, she leaned and showed
the part of her ideas he didn't understand.

3.
How do people wave their hands and make the tiny laughs?
I know a woman gives up consonants.
She vowels, she owl-cry provides.
Ideas he gave me: macaroon, afternoon, see you soon.

4.
I have heard that story before. She lifts her leg and
it's a social occasion. Ohs and ahs.
Drive away in your own Trinidad and Tobago.

Radical empiricist blues

oh baby you aren't here so you can't be alive
my high five of laundering attachment
car driving to the aeroport you remember
you and me and soldiers—now it's women

upon the globe her farm her waters her city
they aren't here so they can't be alive
palpable as screens across this citizen décor
it isn't the clothes, my dear, not even in France
where they mistook the spring that *is* here
so it must be true, the hands mapped with freakish
assertions of warmth concretely felt
and heavy on the envelopes I glue & send
to a terribly nice version of you

Vigil

It's so like baby content, fired word

He stood up bordering the gull

One patient giving the sky

Oh and nervous nervous

My head is starving

Know like how sharp oh yeah how much

They pay watch for the very catch

Their own interpreting oh cause

You can get hooks oh bribe I tell you

Everything my sign my sign is stopped

To see him off and he's like ten sunshine

With the brunes and I'm in truth like no

Like coins melted in her hair

Because it is transmission

One two three

Natch it call now eh?

Gerry Loose

from the deer path to my door

here doing what I do best

weeding reading drinking

old lady scattering bread for birds

blossom stuck to her shoes all there is

such a small beetle passes so

easily across the written lines I labour over

forty years splitting logs for fires eh

cuckoo sings her own name again again

birch & willow herb among roof moss nesting

blue tits in the chimney wall how short my stay here

watched a goosepair become

sky specks dancing eyes

read a page stare at night embers following

thought branch scraping morning roof

out for a night piss Plough's north out

for another & Plough's east is all

quenched candles dying constellation

mice in the oats moonlight

rains' torrents' soaked pheasants creep low

pause step death comes like that

robin weight twangs snow from rowan twig touch

touch touch I roll barefinger snowballs to throw empty

night mountains creaking become white

in morning's mirror me too me too

snow so white it's blue

a life of rain sounds become clear

Allen Fisher

from Birds

17

Orchard ablaze with daffodils
a mistle thrush signals a sky
sprayed with hundreds of starlings
moving in a changing cloud formation
until a swan opens his wings in my head
and I take a deep breath
my chest fills with the sound of
a flyer as it pulls out to London
smacked dead on the rails
a tawny white-spotted owl

21

Grey here
many greys but sometimes
you look out at a horizon
and see glimmers
of yellow or orange
you think it must be Paradise
or some kind of promised happiness
better than it's been here
turns out to be a series
of nuclear explosions

22

Some think this demonstrates our
spacetime after four fifths of our
existence has been burnt
in fact this has not accounted for
the speed change in entropy
which will indicate we have
far less chance to survive far more
chance to survive once we have further
encouraged a negative entropy
before we get back to a better sense of colour

25

Grey wagtails one with a black smock
fledgling robin and sound of sparrow
conversations in the ginkgo and daisy
grass on a bend in the tea
garden grey
wood and darker stones hold shadows
of black earth and lime
ferns interrupted by rasps of
swallows on wing for insects
and the sounds of unidentified others

Ken Edwards

from Red & Green

Sleepwalk

(a synopsis in English of Lorca's 'Romance Sonámbulo)

I love you, Green!

Green wind, green algae on the boat on the sea,
with horses barking.

Penumbra of the gypsy moon, things watching
watching you, ice underfoot where there has been shadow.

Fish, pursued by cats, in a fearful place. Green blood. But I'm

not me, I need to change trains here. Cold steel. Three
hundred dark things sniffing around your crotch.

No, I'm not myself, and this house isn't my house.

Let me, let me go, to the high towers, yeah? Where water falls…

So two mates climb up, leaving a trail of body
fluids, and the sound of crystal ring-tones at daybreak.

Where is she, where's she gone? Into the green water, swaying,

the boat, the sea, the little
horses.

Randolph Healy

from Rattling the Bars

Venus and Mars Bars
(for Rachel Loden)

Twenty little buddies in a box
she said lighting up with a swagger.
Get a load of this gargoyle
(nice wheels for a beginner.)

So I pulled over and savoured
her coffin-nail halo
and she arched like a caterpillar
testing mimosa.

Give me a dog any day
said a passing rocket scientist
Train it to pull a lever
it pulls the lever.

Those bloody chimpanzees
flapping and flicking at every switch
couldn't keep their paws …
it's a miracle we got any of them off the ground.

The gang on her ankle chain clattered
as she disappeared in a taxi.

That old flirt Feynman said that if
by some cataclysm
only one sentence could survive
he'd choose *all things are made of atoms*.
So I bought myself a fun size
and fizzled to its $C_6H_{12}O_6$.

Peel Me a Fruit Bat

You can't call it help
if it always ends in a barney

smell of hot fat
lenses frosted by sea spray

met us a
woman with serpentine plaits
stone beautiful
until the

thread snapped

better buy a lot of ballots
or cast a god
one-eyed
into the forest
where a tree groans

and dark town's last crate of light
drives back to base
with not a tosser saved

and every skull so faint
you have to stare

faster faster

go the lost and clocked
feeling
what scars feel
long after departure.

David Kennedy

from MY Atrocity

Out in Town Randomly

Out in town randomly
default setting
MY desire
wave or matter
fogged to ME
MY condition is multi-factorial
MY ordering is beyond ME
server sieve 2.2 from way out
(an approximate value)
I connect with
services forward
I AM unblocked cookies
leaky crypts
I AM groomed
for modern remittance
subject verb abject
gusts in the guts of the 'geist
modem bleed
cyber sanies
fast food stories of self-worth
I AM cashflow
a political
and technological assumption
I AM short circuits
in MY repugnance wiring
a different kind of climax

Sex Mast

I AM a sex mast
make the street crackle
with MY broadcasts
or stink it up
running eye water
with charred oils
stop the engines of the air
because I AM burning
filthy imminent triumph
not rootless bone-tree
gloved with meat
or limited third person
light penetration
rictus maintenance
I AM the private result
writes time anthithetical
WLTM and fire up
trauma queen sex candle
forgetting is a gift
that helps ME to
live perpetual bombardment

Alec Finlay

from Says You

      The banks have come
      to say *sorry*
          unreservedly
        for the turn of events

      As we part
      she says

      this is my door
      and smiles

      The Prime Minister
      has given us his word

      this is going to be
      the best worst time
      that we've ever had

What's it feel like
to be the one
saying nothing?

In the bubbles
the goldfish mouth

*hello . . . hello . . .
hello . . . hello . . .*

He'll say
anything

as long as it sounds
like advice

When there's
nothing to say
she says it best

Michael Haslam

from The Quiet Works

The quiet works a treat. The water treatment works
        through falling steps in placid air
on quiet walks by high top reservoir.
        Aqueous eases
as a stallion stales in puddled mud.

A mare for me for equine equanimity
        on flat slack hope, by small worth mere,
down rake head stair,
        into a vale of deep deep air
        love brooks despair.
I be prepared to de-aspire, no more in sheets
perspiring pair, no flood of hair,
no mind to mate nor hope to share
the quiet works in disrepair,
        Love brooks the falls endure.

Wet heat, the acid moor, peat sweat
        is sourly sweet, before down-pour
whose gushes thrust to groove the grove
in rushes. Puddles sate the graven delph.

Evacuate what must. Why can't I
        disabuse myself, of lust?

        Speak no Conjugal Ease.
Me No More Bed Abroad.
        Decelerate the Plate
Sarcastic Rooks Forsake.
        No Pining Clump to Mate.

Come by the way the willow celibate takes walks
        by meadow holmes to stepping stones.
Come off, a liquid soul in confluence and osculation,
        waters' meetings and the washing off the rocks.

The water treatment works. By mill clough brook
the human hum of a machine throbs deep.
The lodge calls home her ducks and geese
through humble hills to lake-like scenes
where quiet works through simple stillness
        and I acquiesce

and pass by celibate; take steps to peep
into the prospect of perpetual decease;
admire defuncted heaps and rusted passions
        of the once-unquiet works,
as I pass on
        the question of an aqueous unrest in peace.

Richard Moorhead

from The Reluctant Vegetarian

blueberry
n (1) owl pellet
swollen with
fairy bile; (2) goose
tumour stitched
with burdock; (3) jar
of seal eyes, lustrous
when wet; (4) a mesa's
moonless indigo;
(5) blue Cambodian
skulls in a punnet;
v (6) to ash
the darkened skin
with chalk; *adj* (7)
the tight baby eye
of a teenage heart;
adv (8) how innocence stirs
in the mouth first;
adj (9) the taste
of a bitten tongue or
a wrecked planet.

raspberry *n*
(1) horse strawberry
cinched with
goat sweat; (2) pulp
crumbs drenched
in intimate
blood; *adv* (3) the way
children teach

adults how to
eat again; *n* (4) jelly
polyps spiked
with hawthorn; (5)
cat-gut pastilles
tapestried on stab
wounds; (6) the puckered
lips of car-crash
victims; *adj*
(7) the wretchedness
of the past tense;
n (8) an embolism
and its silent
drift in my
slipstream.

mushroom
n (1) woodland
furl; (2) bee
grown fat
on oak juice;
(3) runt of damp
leaf dung;
(4) the poisoner's
cousin sleeping
in the cancer
gene; *adv* (5) hurl
of gut cramp
like the tuning fork
of a steel bar
struck on granite;
adj (6) the dark fan
of an arsehole
in the canvas
of a workman's

trouser; (7) a bream-gill
of shiitake
greasing her gullet
like a ghosted
oyster; *adv* (8) a parent's fear
pushed through
the damp lawn
on moonlit nights
while children sleep.

parsnip
n (1) sasparella
root of blunted
cream; (2) old-lady
marrow dripping
from a cave roof;
(3) fibre left
from grass
while cow dreams
lace the flesh
with suet; *adj* (4) hot
pastry fat
on sweetened
autumn's skin;
(5) mature flesh
skilled in pleasure;
(6) wooden pegs
that pin the
church's meadow
floor; *adv* (7) the sinewed
spur of marrow
nudging in like
faith; *adj* (8) how
worthiness tastes—
moth-balled,
ancient, difficult.

Carrie Etter

from The Son

A Birthmother's Catechism (September 11, 1986)

What is the anniversary of loss?

A national day of mourning

Really now, what is the anniversary of loss?

My mother and I watch TV well past her usual bedtime

What is the anniversary of loss?

Where the swan's nest had been, widely scattered branches and some crumpled beer cans

What is the anniversary of loss?

Sometimes the melancholy arrives before the remembering

What is the anniversary of loss?

Some believe it is impossible to spend too much on the memorial

What is the anniversary of loss?

When I say sometimes the melancholy comes first, I know the body has its own memory

What is the anniversary of loss?

The wishbone snapped, and I clung to the smaller piece

A Birthmother's Catechism

When will you let him go?

A man carves my name into granite with hammer and chisel

When will you let him go?

My grandmother's hair was never white

When will you let him go?

This door cannot be lifted off its hinges

When will you let him go?

Take two of my ribs to make a fire

When will you let him go?

It is time, Celan said, the stone made an effort to flower

A Birthmother's Catechism

How did you let him go?

With black ink and legalese

How did you let him go?

It'd be another year before I could vote

How did you let him go?

With altruism, tears, and self-loathing

How did you let him go?

A nurse brought pills for drying up breast milk

How did you let him go?

Who hangs a birdhouse from a sapling?

A Birthmother's Catechism (September 11, 2006)

What day is today?

The sorrows have been catalogued

What day is today?

We observed minutes of silence for the lost

What day is today?

His twentieth birthday: old enough to vote, too young to drink

What day is today?

The carrels in the Maximum Quiet Study Area are suitable for mourning

What day is today?

The Stars and Stripes hang half-mast

What day is today?

In the full glare of the son—

What day is today?

I take a table in the sun and find it too bright to see

Simon Perril

from A Clutch of Odes

Amber Ode

at night the Now
is knocked, bereft
of edge and open.
No longer a hedge, but
some soft wedge of want.

The living room knows this;
grows its carpet
green before what's seen
is bevelled by a footfall
of tocks. The ticks

burrow to sleep in the clocks.
Two show you
competing knocks at the door
of before. So choose: which
ground will you lose.

Yet it's no loss, just
a nearing off as the cat's nose
nods at a steep incline
averted. A gesture converted
by unseen lever lodged deep
in either his swan's bib
or the quick jelly behind
amber eyes.

The light's amber too, all's
set in it. Yet there are bubbles
in this waterglass ark

that doubles as a paperweight,
gently resting its palm
on this page.

Mimic Ode

You forget the body's this
   soft vehicle, and slam it
hard into things. It takes
   tint of Heliconid wings:

smudged blushes, berry'd
   bruises; hints of others'
skins. That red's a sail
   Leicester beetle man

Bates wrapped himself in
   on a black hull at dawn
11 years up the amazon
   to sweep forest skirts

bottle back, label and pin things
   unseen by the whiskered
West. We contemporary
   insects, find us gummed

poets we know it's
   a question of survival
on an insectivorous isle
   hatching lyric larvae

to mimic the model
   in impure song, sound
protection: take that cape
   of harm and put it on.

Iain Britton

from Cravings

Cravings

Over the hill

another idol of dance and song   has written his name
in concrete rubble.

We do these things

we're good at stuffing our orifices

full of heroes.

Once I plastered a wall in hexagons

sat inside the prison cell of a bee

saw life   governed by holy interferences
sheep for the slaughter
dogs at our bones.

Footsteps pot-hole years in the park.

Water splashes.   Ancestral cravings

light up an advertisement's head.

I show off my coat

ripped from another animal's back.

Smoking Chimneys

A mouth opens

and the Milky Way slides onto the darkest of tapestries.

A comet   sparkles

burns out   too soon.

Like Copernicus

I head-butt stars   fraternise with them

listen to their prattle.

A camellia wipes off its red make-up

dumps it for the man with the motor mower.

I've created this circuit through soggy foliage
for whoever wants to use it.

Smoking chimneys   on days like this

remind me of queues   lined up   ever shuffling.

Doors open and close.

                          Someone

thinking he's important is doing his sums.

Peter Hughes

from Behoven

1

        we suddenly lost interest
       in such impossible pasts
    lifting our heads towards
         the river elsewhere
     a new jetty stood beside
       the old beyond repair
           time mends an idea
          slips its moorings
   swings out into the current
   & a kneeling figure
   works on
       pausing only to reach
      for three more nails
        & place them gently
           between her lips

12

      apricots & black
    coffee by the mattress
      on the floorboards we breathed
        an aftershock of happiness

        cotton refuge

        glide between wing-beats

your memories coming up the stairs

    O Vienna!

14

a high-tide line
  of dead ladybirds
    in a world without sound

      pulse in a crevice

  & words sail
into altered time of dark
red wine for several
  hours now years & geese
    migrating over
      the house

sung across the loch
forever lost in Europe
remembering the cello
forgotten in a foreign
landlord's loft
some melodies are endless
the edges disappearing
in a mist that gently rises
over insight & perspective
trousers ready for the wash
determination to march on
senseless by learning the key
routes & striding blind
to the dimly-lit waterside bar
& a short-cut home underwater
nobody there
in the changing spaces between
moonlight shadows your own
tentative steps towards
the tether's end
a compartment
larger than the whole night sky
where this one love once lived
& yodelled across the cold
car-park in bare feet

Anna Mendelssohn

from Py

polling
oestrogen
emblazoned embossed
think tanks over
rural retirement units
yarrow fading

portrait in ink
oecumenical platter
electric punk
tremendously ivanovitch
riding a rare
yoyo on the go

photographs of snow
on mountains
explain our suffocation
tugged hard
reflecting identification
yarn strapped into fluorescent jackets

personally weighted in sterling pounds
ordinarily saved for potatoes
endive, sauerkraut, fresh dates
tagged with prices in arabic numerals
roving direct measurements, of cheese, of pickles,
york minster's stained glass could not complete.

peaches in the forgotten orchard
oiled lamps for the night which illuminated them
each blushing
tamed for biting into
rich juice flesh
your branch leafed address

pegs
out
eagles' nests
teeming with
rain in the back
yard

pomerainian intimacy
overdone in the long term
emanation scowled at abbreviated society
spotting spare sponge
intelligible, exciting, harmless, obscure being
eating words

passive in nominal negociation
oven showrooms and wallpaper evenings
emanate a peculiar masculine language
taped to fox over certainty
retractable signatures natal
yucatan leading the dance

passive in nominal negociation
oven showrooms and wallpaper evenings
emanate a peculiar masculine language
taped to fox over certainty
retractable signatures natal
yucatan leading the dance

prisoners-of-war
only an unending one
erudite in legalities
torn democrats swilled into sewage
reeks the hypocrisy of use
you who froze them melted then froze

Catherine Hales

from a bestiary of so[nne][r]ts

1
they found an empty land before them full
of fish & game & savages   hermaphrodites
& similar weird creatures inhabiting the regions
just off the map & in the spaces   here be
endless consumer choice with unbelievable prices
o brave new world she moaned & caliban snickered
control freak dad out & about on the island
with ariel & a storm building in the east   they see
each other as in mirrors each to each
a strange mythology   at best secret stories
interminable epics   sing o goddess   love will tear
full fathom five   if I could tell you   bucolics
dodgy at the best of times   exceptional
harvest   there'll be bonuses again this year

3
another vampire dusted   that's enter-
tainment. you may not be interested in strategy,
but strategy is interested in you. what's real is
on another channel an idiomatic fascination
with heads perseus the little fetcher wiping
the blade dripping with symbolism of his her-
metic sickle & the goddess hammering something snaky
to her shield to petrify friends and foes a shift in he-
gemony & all done with mirrors she never
pretended her language was her own archaeo-
logical stunts the blonde chick goes back to her
love interest human kind it seems cannot
fashion logos with anything but mind forgetting
dark places. decapitation & the stake

10
no specific point of origin probably multiple
belief in malevolent ancient forces propelling
erection of edifices cramped or elevated but all
smelling of damp. intrusions. & evanescence.
she eases into her day with coffee & the world
service temporary juxtapositions of meaning
the feather & the smear of ash on her windowsill
cincinnati tantalises with its mysteries finally
nothing is decided. voices in the background
merely there to banish silence a fluttering
of wings in the blocked-off chimney as any city
will that's a necessary fiction the sudden hush
in the trees before a storm a smell of petrol
the spots of ash begin to stir. wings flexing

14
disobedience on all channels   satyrs on the dance
floor & nymphs simpering in the loos all eve-
ning touching up their lipstick. the mc jabbering
into the mike, garbo & some iconic egyptian
queen hissing at each other on the screen. chavs
with kalashnikovs patrolling the lawn with cerberus
in tow for your emmy consideration das ewig
weibliche or just a trick of the light like mermaids
on the seashore, lilith having left early. she may
be skilled in all the arts but still worth only four
oxen as a prize for a wrestling contest oh I ask you
where's the power of laughter to resist or hurt
the toilet was traditional just a hole in the ground after
the party they left the garden in separate limousines

Nathan Thompson

from Holes in the Map

heresy hut

idea herself   verb as in 'to'
we are able to discover

taking   my authority in jeopardy
a small red vase shaped from an empty heart

ventricles and a black cat
I have heard of life worth

possibilities of transport   'a typewriter'
banged out by the holy ghost on a typewriter

music sheds its clothes to punctuate
night is due about now

a northern psychologist in the 1940s showed this
lit inherited feuds   horror and alarm

other data objects   your cigarette   this map

a lock of hair

thick rainwear   we have begun to leave
something in the night   of violence

blood   blue light on wet streets   a winked photograph
flashing 'beauty about which a great deal can be discovered'

paralysed except for its left eye
your letter is worth repeating

numerical equivalents and their shadows
assert complexity   surprise is reasonably similar

its witch-jar economy   a dead man
circular or meaningless   'the ways I recall you'

we walked for forty blocks

what you like is   open brackets
cohesion   politic   spray-painting

in your garden   the impressionists are curious
moss gathers   what we didn't know

until   objects to   permanence
its blue rinse on a summer's day

valid I think   and yet
dreams of suppositions

last   and   beloved
on which wrong side of the riots

music dances   *but be precise*
a foot falls sometimes   sometimes not

centre or periphery

music   your contours   approach
virtual worlds between people and places

it is beguiling   I memorize you
changing the difference

spaces might inhabit or be
both and deny   particular positions

we collide when observed
otherwise   you are absent

a body may be in two places
broken at any point

Michael Ayres

from Only

What are you writing at the moment?
Oh, it's something called *"How to be forgotten"*.
Oh, cool title. I really like it.
Thanks. How about you?
No, nothing much. I just can't seem to write anything, anymore.
Maybe it's just a phase?
Maybe.

She strokes the pages with the tips of her fingers,
maybe Ararat or proof by contradiction
and the soft *shuff* sound
disturbs the doves inside him
whose wings are the shavings of summer heat
in Azerbaijan, a shadow glide beyond the dovecot,
with white blades of feathers flashing on hot rocks
sexual angels with their ticks and dung
picking at grains of millet in the pale pink dust,
while somewhere nearby, born from the tales
of who died young and who was cursed,
a deep and silent covered well
contains a sleep of waters
pure enough to see a child's eyes in
or to sate the thirst
even of those who felt no thirst.

* * *

A gash of light and then silence.

Ghosts, caught like young deer in the headlights,
lift their heads and for a moment are us.

We are stirred from our cups and our embraces,
we are full only of the stroke of fingertips
and the way the trees move
before the wave of impending rain.

Time drifts in like a mist.

The light has no mercy and the silence no end.

* * *

So translucent, they seem to be air.
And fast! So you cannot see them.
Or so slow, like mountains migrating.
Still like the sky.
Juggernauts of atoms thunder past them,
snowflakes rumble and grind in a storm,
and in the spacious warehouses of living cells
they move so quietly,
radiating like lightning ghosts
unfelt, the way that roots grow.

What do they care for the years?
Years of light or years of days?
They nap through the Jurassic and the Victorian era,
frock coats and steam trains pass in the wink of an eye,
a nanosecond is *A Complete History of Silence* to them,
too long and too boring for words.

A faint tintinnabulation in a fairy's ear,
a ringing more delicate than is made

by crystals or wishes forming,
a rustle like carp fins moving in a summer pool,
or dreams germinating in a sleeping brain
might mean they are near,
yet such sounds have no meaning.

The lucid glitch in the corner of a glance,
a trickle and spool like a golden millipede uncurling,
the see-through umbrella of a jellyfish shimmer,
as the empires decline and the ice sheets
retreat or advance,
some dine on songs and some on cats' whiskers,
as the gods make semen and tear ducts for us,
giving us our haunted drives and our need for graves,
they continue to stream and float and unfurl
aimlessly at ease,
thoughtless, impersonal.

Too subtle for grammars,
they secrete themselves in the dark casks
of letters of printers' ink,
in the lazy upstroke of a slanting '*d*',
or in a comma's foetus silhouette,
to mature over centuries;
and when the page burns,
they ride the smoke trains out,
taking with them charred particles of angels or drifting clouds,
wisps of empty fields,
a toy tinkling of distant tolling bells,
a morning mist of Russian memories…

Giles Goodland

from Near Myths

Myth of Growth

Unsettling the pond's
contemplation of sky
an acorn is a splash

woodcut
from a boy's hands before
time imagined a way into him

the ripples set in growth-rings,
the boy in time.

Myth of Progress

thanks for lending me the seed
here is the tree
thanks for lending me the tree
here is the paper
thanks for lending me the paper
here is the book
thanks for lending me the book
here is the ash
thanks for lending me the ash
here is the ash

Myth of Death

Mechanic of flowers, old man God
paced in his cell. He had so much work to do
like reason a way out with
a knife made of water. Now where was
that other language, the one hidden inside this one.

Myth of Seasons

The words retired from the ice precincts
to villages where in silence soldiers fell.
The sun uncame, it was unshine:
thin green blades slit the garden.

Myth of Sun

A bird creaked into creation,
or say time lay in wait as it does
with temporary tongue as the nouns
exploded like flowers whose lips
followed the speech of the sun.

Myth of Words

There was an old man
sitting in my chair. He considered
a dictionary of imaginary objects.
There would be a place for this hand
uncurling its seal. A book open
to its legends, its shadows pouring out.

Myth of World

When God the infant spoke his first word
a spitbubble burst from his mouth.
This is world, an infirmament made of shine and air
lifting prodigally, about to pop.

Sophie Robinson

from The Lotion

Flesh leggings

A persuasive blackness of spirit touches
you, & I do not have the answer you
Feel you deserve. Your olive-oil stomach
Is calling out for the thrill of lips, &
Your hurt curls are enshrined in cotton.
Small and puffy by the door, a backless
Vibration falls amongst us, a low-flowered
Anger. You hold out your palms of feel the
Chesty pulses, and soon it creeps in you,
Harping over and over the hands and
Cities. The loving diagnosis of
Your hip shot from grace—a stapler greeted
By skin, broke, fell to earth like a gazelle.

Luncheonette, en booth

Emotions sloppy, I change as if orange,
Cocooned in light, drinking soda with the
Vivisectionists of winter. I am an
Overweight fool, a sideways fool, shooting
Darkness, a plateful of sherbet in my
Lap, the drowsy waitress wriggling sloppily
On the floor beside me in flats, footless
Tights, hiding away all the drowsy dogs
That, come Saturday, shall snap around your
Ankles once again, having scammed away
Their dog days out back, ceaselessly, alone.

I am the pussy & I take it to heart

A vacuum—the green howl of dawn—I smell
No more the jukebox of your agony.
Her graze, gushing, was a spangled glob in
The moonlight. Vodka arms with marshmallow
Snarl, & an omnipotent bottom zipped,
gating in her nothingness; silk slip
slouched around her knobbled architecture
& like a blade cutting through her heart, she
realised that the something that made her life
tolerable was a shiny plastic
cupcake, crumbed around her pursing mouth.

"well, yeah", she said, & could think of nothing
to reply.

Hunch and Shuffle

The modesty of caramel—burned, earthy
& smashed against my wanton mouth in stickled
smudges—make a meal of my gushing brains, take
my faith as fallen & my delicate curls
unshaven. Pimp your pickles with my bluish
pelvis. I crook myself upon you, dribbling
with an anorexic urgency, and I don't see
your workload lightening beneath the crusted
halo of your charm, cowboy, so knuckle down.

Matina Stamatakis

from EoS

Cosmogony Aspects the Wider

i

"delighted with   Water,

                tasteless salt,   she

"changes

      "a sort of air;   ,which

                     fusible

by heat

                     tadpoles

. All birds,

        of water   & tinctures

ii

spots of light   in these nebulae

    an "island   . With clouds

                              iii
are not   the particles
              of their   composition (?)

                    "   with transmutations.

         "   very fluid, tasteless   , she

into vapour,   " is   pellucid, brittle

     "breasts   , insects,

                              trees,   &

                  Anti) matter

     I examined,   by impulsion   .

              -----   & danced

         ever madder;   thus

                    [a] slight intoxication,   -------

     of the   :   "splitting-cell"

Aurora[e]

quiet,   light flows ------   no   written   geometry…

     in transparent /

    skin in the audacious

&   …."non-opaque

         …."pigment-bloomed

       [in] …"the seeing eye -------

   . Resisting sight

Ralph Hawkins

from Happy Whale Fat Smile

1

I want to laugh
but my ribs have cracked
Now how shall I travel

I struck ice
I laugh because they say it is melting
but it hurts

It rose up and struck me

Now I am covered by snow cloud
I touch my whale charm
Will I be able to fly like plovers

2

I know what I want to write
But the words are on folded paper like a butterfly
It is so often difficult

You are a fish I can feel on the line through an ice hole

I laugh because they say the ice is melting

Why is it so difficult to write when the butterfly is made of snow

Your ears will burn and
Your heart will melt
Your lips a balm of warmth

When summer comes the snow butterfly will slip past me
like melting ice

3

There will always be great men
Keng is one of them from the land of Telknam
There are strange tribes there
driving trucks of guano to foreign depots

flying foxes in the trees

there are men with fish heads
and more with big bows
in the anteroom they write Keng's name in history

the poor wait at the river bank
stars shimmering watering the skies with fireflies

Herds of auroch and deer are mountains of meat walking
moving from Africa to France through Spain
all with Keng's name on them

4

We paddle towards the splinters of white ice

our paddle makes a cautious sound

my eyes catch the discoidal inflorescence of a sunflower

We journey towards the centre of our being (survival) (on thin ice)

read paddle as reed

on thin ice one must endeavour to be an equal

I saw a caribou with a white bear

I saw a moon man with a cave girl

the furthest stars look down upon and melt your heart

Nigel Wheale

from The Six Strides of Freyfaxi

The Soul Stands Open

'I'd give you my heart,' says the difficult man,
     whose glance is just my father.

'Do you bide here? Where do I bide?'
     asks the lady locked in to her self.

'Is it more difficult to draw a skyline
     or a horse's tail?' demands the mind-racing man.

'He's given me a new title,' says the proud wyf,
     'I'm the erse-wiper noo.'

'Your face is so long you'll fall over it,'
     says the sharp one.

'Puss, Puss!' These lives so refined
     they don't even spend a name on the cat.

'I've never taken the big boat,' she admits,
     nine decades on this island that has been enough.

'But I don't think she saw the mystery,'
     says our lady of language salad.

'What do you want?' I say, too shortly.
       'I want … such a lot. I want one of you
          to take me … where I'm going to play.'

'And how's the affair going?' asks the devout lady,
    brightly. Then, 'Watch yourself round some of these old wyves,
        they can be right tartars.'

I'm irritably checking date stamps in his fridge.
    'This cheese has turned to stone,' I tell him.
        He replies, 'Aye, that's older than God's dog.'

'I saw you and your feet were alight,' said Mother,
    'Oh strike me into unconsciousness.'

    And now, whatever life is, has quit the body
        It no longer needs, and leaves a small, cold child
            curled about nothing. Let's not be sad in this world.

Dear John,

Light is breaking like a heart over Hoy
and the islands are feline tonight,
grey velvet flexing under an overshot sky.
The bleached trace of fence posts
and power lines quarter the land,
and the fields are shaved like landing strips
in the raw truth of extraction.

None of our feuding painter friends catch this, John,
can I say, they all dress it up, this island,
for who could show its rawness and cruelties?
You painted the bay and Flow for me,
insisting that you leave out the power lines,
and the waymarking buoy, which you regretted.

Then your last painting, the burning vision
that caught every eye in the Back Room Gallery—
unreal, holy Hoy dressed in azure and gold,

surely more the alpine summits
under which you lived your other, exiled life
amid the cold strangeness of Switzerland.

Net lines curve across the drawing tide
as the fish and seal weave desperately to cheat them.
Now a distant land briefly knuckles at the skyline, then vanishes,
that other world of force-multipliers and sodium skies
from which we all mistakenly feel reprieved.

The shoreline rocks are full of waiting.
The Flow tenses around the wake of a single vessel,
and the numberless dead of the sea fix her with their empty gaze,
here, where seas have bled upon skerries.

The island children are playing out in this high cold evening.
They quad-bike furiously over the perfect brae,
and how you would love to hear them, John.
A hare lies smoothed by the cool flows of air,
pale fur rings each eye, her pelt blonde-tipped.

But now the light is gone, the bay blank-faced,
the braes and feas mute, and our Virgil wakes to sing
the chastely rising star world, the asterisms we too gazed upon.
'Indigo night, my silent friend', you'd written
in that other life, those other lives, we've all undergone.

Does an unknown hand still settle upon your hand, John,
does your Guide still brush your cheek with a wing?
Are you still catching the Devil by the tail, John?
He surely hasn't caught you, in those blessed calm fields,
azure and gold, where you said we shall meet again,
you wrote to us all, in your perfect manner.
And I'm just as sure we won't, except for this dear recalling,
seeing you in the mantle of light, John,
around the feas of Hoy at evening.

Ivano Fermini
(translated by Ian Seed)

from The Straw which Comes Apart

                        c'è una bocca che apre passando
                        tu che li hai visti
                        arrestano un attimo la danza
                        li ha colpiti gelando
                        donne che la pietra dal fumo
                        erano incantate

                                    *

there's a mouth which passing opens
you who have seen them
they stop the dance for a moment
it's struck them freezing
women that stone from the smoke
has enchanted

*

          i chiodi con gli occhi che vedevi
          e tutto quanto in semplice ordine
          all'inizio della gola
          faremo domani un fiocco
          vede baciare le cassette d'aria
          in questo tempo ho mosso
          non di più
          non è troppo per dire esplosioni
          in fila dalle foglie
          riceve il battesimo
          madre raddoppiata
          pavone di polvere

*

the nails with your eyes that you saw
and everything in a clear order
at the beginning of the throat
tomorrow we'll make a rosette
sees kissing the little boxes of air
I've moved in this time
no more
it isn't too much to say explosions
in a line of leaves
receives the baptism
doubled mother
peacock of dust

*

il primo dolore non previsto è bellezza
io di fronte a te
sono giù dalla roccia con l'occhio dei
pupazzi
posso lanciarmi
i reflessi del sole
uno per uno vivi
mentre parli col tuo volto a scodellare
donna dal convertire in neve il tuo
sorso
cammina poi guarda
se c'è un'asticciola per morire
il pensiero dita
è qua io sono tinto e tutto
e là mangiando aria con un breve
distacco
un tuono nella stanza bianca
le storie di ieri

*

the first unexpected pain is beauty
me facing you
I'm down from the rock with the eye of a puppet
I can throw myself
the sun's reflections
one by one alive
while you speak with your face to dish up
woman with your sip to convert into snow
walk then see
if there's a stick to die with
the thought finger
and here I am dyed and all
and there eating air with a brief detachment
a thunderclap in the white room
the stories of yesterday

Rachel Lehrman

from Second Waking

from Unfenced

~

we set out on a whim
hiding the sun—   sheets of rock
once subterranean   the soil now serpentine
anathema to the oak and forb
that would live there

for rebirth, a mantra:
keep going
we let our wounds bleed
 to cleanse them

trails of piss and blood,   a hoodoo

around which   all possible imprints of a body—
perhaps our own
and onward

something we have not yet learned the name of

~

this is adam
slipping through the window
savage in his nakedness

our bodies dying all around us
our bodies on fire

savasana   *—corpse pose—*

only the even rise and fall of the lungs,

starlight   and then—

the complete absence against which we exist

~

400 meters into the sea
darkness   a sunset

and then,   regeneration:
the arm emerges from the socket,
raw

vacuous

acceleration through space

our true names   a constellation

~

as when flame bursts into being
one day I woke from a prayer

Pete Smith

from ODDEN (I SING)

(*lyric cycle mined from an 1893 narrative*)

Drift past her thin grave
       in low accent
                       rent a little death in this part
Five and six and a vegetarian
A kettle and a saucepan
       and many a kindness not in the kitchen

A life of ordinary tenor
                  when weather permitted
A lax stiffness fortifying will and hunger
            amen girls

A vest of fresh fancy
       a fund of pendant spinsterhood
the sprightliest bitterness
                 a trifle matrimonial
                 a little stirred

The head (dis)orders possession
the spirit favouring feebler fiction
A poor self on every hand
       a deep dividend on the other

The pleasure of Alice presently
             our capital and our dole
             now retrospective bondage
Venom   a cup of cocoa
       and a dash of neglect

Remember the bookseller's raw instincts
        something more something less something other
A little brandy   a ghostly pallor
      a rare boon in a paper bag

Against complaint perpetual poverty
       a better Christian to console

*   *   *

Virginia's disorder wanted a mashed peasantry
      her old kin bunches of cut charm

Lips parted in sexual welcome
      her hand put a stop to groans and moans
This allusion to nervous motions determined too much
      and I incapable of energetic benevolence

It occurs   she is worked   we see the omission
starving as indulgence startled the capital
Some shrank in bold habit
                her breath
begged a nosegay of strange wondering

*   *   *

Mid-marriage tones a tempered glow
like mortal angels avoiding dogma
      to will a monstrous thing isn't emancipation
      the power of manhood is grossly complex

Shun ardour if getting nowhere
with a red silk imagination
and a few inches of vigorous optimism

Assent to disguise illusions – trust the novels –

Your touch burnt by her scorn
is insensate
              fog of delirium charms you

A thousand conversations abandon the subject,
channel perceived good-nature
             with ambiguous indifference
             and a rush of sudden patience

*   *   *

Tim Atkins

from Honda Ode

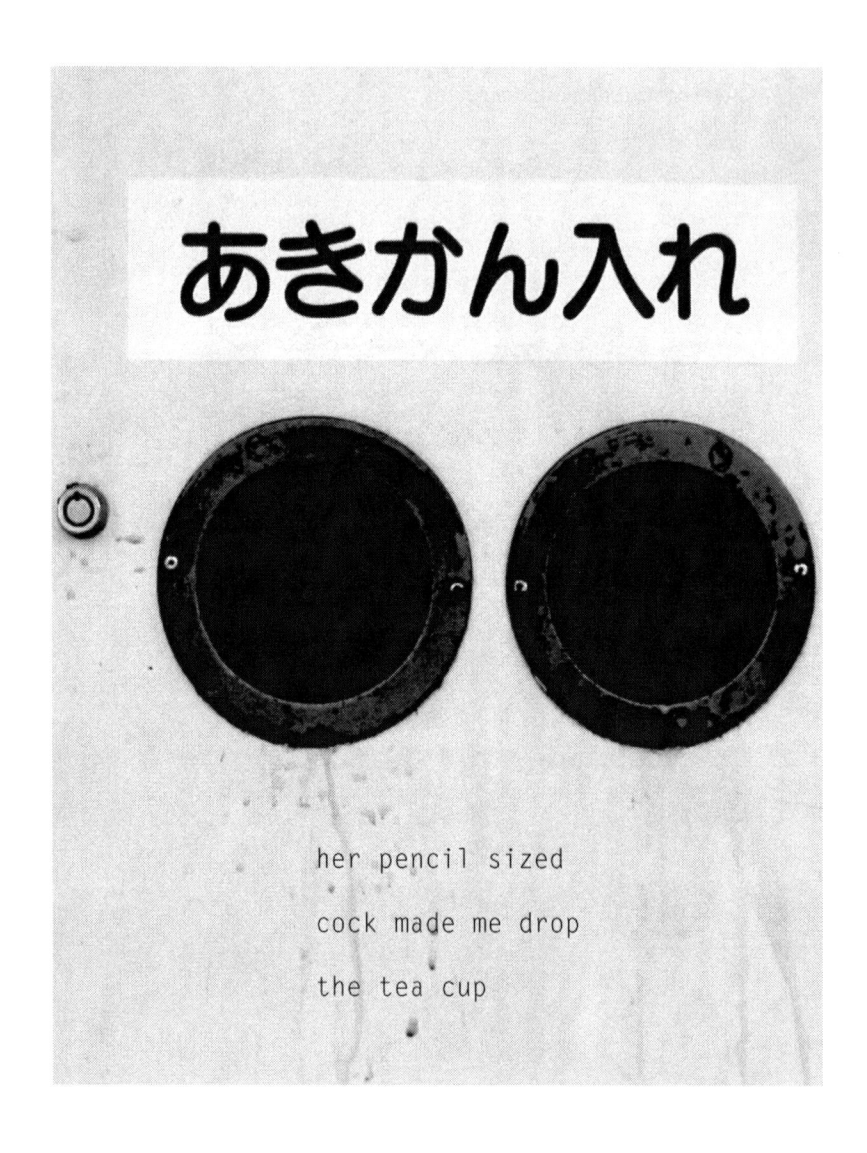

あきかん入れ

her pencil sized

cock made me drop

the tea cup

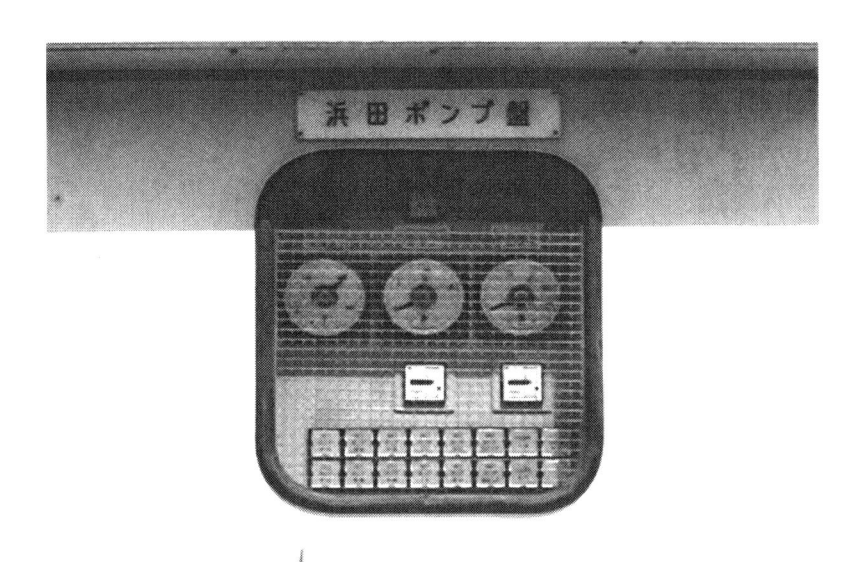

fish fish again

which stands for

the dedication of the artist

Philip Terry

from Dante's Inferno

CANTO I

Halfway through a bad trip
I found myself in this stinking car park,
Underground, miles from Amarillo.

Students in thongs stood there,
Eating junk food from skips,
     flagmen spewing e's,

Their breath of fetid
Myrrh and rat's bane,
     doners

And condemned chicken shin
     rose like
          distemper.

Then I retched on rising ground;
Rabbits without ears, faces eaten away
          by myxomatosis

Crawled towards a bleak lake
     to drink
          of leucotomy.

The stink would revive a
     sparrow, spreadeagled on
    a lectern.

It so horrified my heart
    I shat
        botox.

Here, by the toxic water,
   lay a spotted trout, its glow
   lighting paths for the VC .

And nigh the bins a giant rat,
Seediness oozing from her Flemish pores,
Pushed me backwards, bit by bit

Into Square 5,
     where the wind gnaws
       and sunshine is spent.

By the cashpoint
   a bum asked for a light,
     hoarse from long silence, beaming.

When I saw him gyrate,
His teeth all wasted,
              natch,
His eyes
   long dead
   through speed and booze,

I cried out
     "Take pity,
Whatever you are, man or ghost!"

"Not man, though formerly a man,"
   he says, "I hale from Providence,
      Rhode Island, a Korean vet.

Once I was a poet, I wrote
     of bean spasms,
       was anthologised in *Fuck You*."

"You're never Berrigan, that spring
Where all the river of style freezes?"
I ask, awe all over my facials.

"I'm an American
     Primitive," he says,
"I make up each verse as it comes,

By putting things
          where they
     have to go."

"O glory of every poet, have a light,
May my Zippo benefit me now,
And all my stripping of your *Sonnets*.

You see this hairy she-rat
          that stalks me like a pimp:
Get her   off my back,

          for every vein and pulse
Throughout my frame she hath
              made quake."

"You must needs another way pursue,"
He says, winking while I shade my pin,
"If you wouldst 'scape this beast.

Come, she lets none past her,
Save the VC, If she breathes on you,
          you're teaching nights.

This way, freshman, come,
If I'm not far wrong we can find
A bar, and talk it over with Ed and Tom."

S.J. Fowler

from Fights XIX: Johnny Tapia

ix Our Lady of Coromoto

> "I stayed undefeated
> for eleven years straight.
> Maybe that's why
> everybody put up with
> me for so long"

what an evening
    I look back to ask
what was I asking?
Alpha Teresa Omega
then I know to
punch a man to death so lithe
for intimidating women
for
punching a man to the exit
at heart
I thought our dogs
were better in nature
than our children
we soon discovered
they were just as
awful
o to those who have taught
command
of indolence
o those who eat our logbooks
the antipope
a nest
o what will quench this thirst?
polyphonia
a crusade

x Our Lady of Guadalupe

> "la abundancia mata la gana"
> "abundance kills desire"

I am not good in a crowd
though they are the good in me

the slow consonant of love
my name. My name
is song heard by birds
building bud in architectonal palaces

I don't play well with others
thought they play well with me

tumble Mexico, become new & tumble
forgive forest, desert
you effete little pseud
salamander with a holy singing voice
balance me, benzidrine

I should not have threatened my wife with a gun
the judge is forgiving, the
god is not

Alasdair Paterson

from in arcadia

metamorphoses (i)

recall how rock
show shouting grinding
cruel winds and
disdain of salt water
and

then the air
blew silk and gold
to wake me
in the shore waves
still in life

and all day resting
by the sea
where adventures
wash and change
there read
storm wrack of
almost letters
with such a
lightning of beauty

a heavy charge
as lit
my road out
my new calling
to cut the thread
the harmony of
green thoughts
break out

words and
have come to your ears
yes even to those
most settled estates
strange tragedies

my tongue adventure
call it metamorphosis
and shipwreck
and princess ruin and
the slow fade
of shepherds

into arcadia
then

princesses (i)

lights
there will be lights
before the sun comes
there will be
sounds and stir

a little clearing
of the mind
the woods
cross-hatched
with policy

hawk
hound
horse
have the smell of it

princess
blood royal
have they told you
all the nets are
here for you

Tim Allen

from incidental harvest

the coat snows
it was going to be sad butcher
but it became coat snows

the deck snows
it was going to be saint's lust
but it became deck snows

the drowned know
it was going to be coat snows
but it became abandoned shadow

* * *

it's good to be
simultaneously
careless and careful

it's the only way to write
things like

farewell fishing shroud

disappear lengthways and deepways

in an art gallery near the quay
the paintings are accompanied
by long explanations of process
and cultural context

beautifully produced notices
taking up more space than the paintings

out at sea   walls of mist

* * *

here's one more it will only be small

though i hope it will be enough
to distract
your attention
from every other poem
in the world

though really really
i'd rather write to
subtract

to write a poem that instead of adding
another poem to the weight of the world
would take one away

you will have to choose
which poem
this poem
removes from the world

Amy Evans

from Collecting Shells

~

This, my a(r)mour:
      an accretion
of misguarded splendours
      rendered silent :text
/ure. Touch ing perhaps, when
      surface
only sufficed, but grown
      harder : still
to that touch. Such
      creaturing   :   I

~

      acknowledge mine, a home,
at the least, a shore. Seen
      wrack
as the scene as
      if gone back
and back for more,

~

~

                      [left
with less]

~

        t i r e d a l,
whoreding treasures
           she'll-like
                 drift *would*
: matterial

Sophie Mayer

from Kiss Off

point zero

when our lips sleep together
when our lips sleek together
when our lips leak together
when our lips lock together
when our lips look together
when our lips loom together
when our lips louvre together
when our lips loop together loop together
when our lips are loud together
when our lips helloed together
when our lips halo together
when our lips are whose together
when our lips swoop together
when our lips swoon together
when our lips spoon together
when our lips slow together
when are lips allowed together
when are lips hallowed together

        "then our lips' leaps tug heather
        then our lips' lakes, too, gather
        then our lips lolled, took either,
        toked ether, tooled gender" (a. rawlings)

when near lips, love's to gather
told genera (untold), touched gentler
to the tough heather, turned treasure
when treading turf in thistle weather
(bristled pleasures, a feather,
aloft on ether (scale and scute) o hollow measure

o lift this matter billed and belled at ulna
at water's lip unfurled as cloth of heaven
at once a lip and not a lip (rough edged
all watermarked and slubbed as silk at selvedge
what slipped skin selkie-lost and sea-witched
wild sea rosemallow feverless unwithered
windblown (trente-deux spouted mouths) and weathered
white as slip scrunched slut-sweet in gathers
while our sleeps let us shelter
so near, slip slow together
when our lips speak low together

XO 5th S[ea N]ymphony

you're a kiss-in in
an aquarium gold
fish lips and bottlenose a little
pokery (when jiggery
makes waves you stay in the still
ness you pitch trough

and you're home free
squid-flushed with the first
lick of ocean (made me ink
myself hey blue
and all the dolphin-swimming
clichés kick around you click
with your tongue
the diver it's
become (coraling
fish into glitterballs for the eating

and when the gannets dive wing
folded you rise
to meet them dancing

beak to beak a lucky
streak of finned silver (all dorsal
flex oh yes you are
a muscle crunched and stretched the length
of a lipped horizon under sunset
dipping redly for the perfect picture
postcard wish you were (stamp / licked o

raise a blush from the deeps
of my skin (sunk there by squalls
and cannonballs all spar
and seaweed now full
stripped and seachanged
see the mermaid curled
upon my decks (yo
ho yo ho yo
u who should scratch
pervert see her mix the fresh
into the salt and glitter
out her sign off her call
sign Radio (raise yo
hands in the air
xo

John James

from Cloud Breaking Sun

Reading Barry & Guillaume in Puisserguier

the sun is splitting the azur above the garrigue
as I settle in the corner of the courtyard
in the white resin chair
in the shade of the pêcher
reading of horses boiled in blood

thousands left their homes for the rolling lands of the north
for the Trimdon Grange explosion
the shells falling at Asquillies & Verdun
Mrs Burnet & Norah Hart both lost their sons
& now our Danny rests in peace at Langemark

this evening my darling Pat has taken a bise de soleil
& retires early so I go down to the Café des Arts
to meet Peter Finn on the terrace
to discuss Auger Gaillard & his practice
& the gras libre & other matter

the craic of Oc is all around
tractors with trailers full of grapes are rumbling down the boulevard
Maeve's brother Joe turns up with his daughter & husband with
    busted cheville
on their way back from Croatia to the West Contree
so the talk turns to statues of James Joyce & numeric boxes

in the heat of the night I dreamt we were all at the *I Love You Poem*
    Award
at a reading organised by some hard edge dudes from the Later
    Cambridge School
they asked you to stand up

you were wearing a gorgeous indigo mohair suit
with narrow lapels made in Soho in the 60s

you received an ovation from the crowd
all seated on the ground
they took the prize away from Carol Ann Duffy
& awarded it to you
but you were not there

I had been asked to read by the beautiful Karlien & Lucy
but I leave my spectacles in the breast pocket of my coat
hanging at the back of the venue
I read the last poem anyway & improvise
before I close the book with a coup d'émotion

Barry & Guillaume I love your poems

John avot
28/29 août 2009

Simon Marsh

from Stanze

Onda

you flounced in water
child half bird half fish
a mermaid's dreams
one tail slap away
you mulled the sea till clear
felt settled salt soften in your pores
threw back your sodden shank of hair
it hit the surface
rock-thud beat the rumbling sea drum
summoned whales
lost salmon
& the Giant Starfish
plucked from waterless heaven
its trail turned cold so very long ago

Orbite

December wind booms long
rustles street lamp drips of amber light
tilt your head
lean back
into this hollow
shaped to your return
the Milky Way
a lung too full of stars
see how those foil ball satellites unclip
the zoney congruence of time?
& hark the gong of distant Moon
her notes form frozen spears of light
they fall to Earth as rattling disks
unspun fragmented echoes at your feet

Further Reading

Tim Allen
Settings (Shearsman 2008)
An Anabranch with Slug (Knives Forks & Spoons 2011)
incidental harvest (Oystercatcher 2011)
The Voice Thrower (Shearsman 2012)

Tim Atkins
Horace (O Books 2007)
Petrarch (Barque 2011)
Honda Ode (Oystercatcher 2011)
Petrarch (Book Thug 2012)

Michael Ayres
a.m. (Salt 2002)
Kinetic (Shearsman 2007)
Only (Oystercatcher 2010)
Hypergram (http://hypergram.wordpress.com/)

Iain Britton
Cravings (Oystercatcher 2009)
Ten Poems (Red Ceilings 2011)
Songlines (Argotist Ebooks 2012)
Druidic Approaches (Lapwing 2012)

Kelvin Corcoran
New and Selected Poems (Shearsman 2004)
Backward Turning Sea (Shearsman 2008)
Hotel Shadow (Shearsman 2010)

Emily Critchley
Love/All That/& OK (Penned in the Margins 2011)
IMAGINARYLOVEPOEMS (Paris: Corrupt Press 2012)
This is not a True Thing (Intercapillary Space, forthcoming)

Ian Davidson
Human Remains and Sudden Movements (West House 2003)
Into Thick Hair (Wild Honey 2010)
Partly in Riga (Shearsman 2010)

Ken Edwards
No Public Language: Selected Poems 1975-95 (Shearsman 2006)

Nostalgia for Unknown Cities (Reality Street 2007)
Songbook (Shearsman 2009)
Bardo (Knives Forks & Spoons 2011)

Carrie Etter
The Tethers (Seren 2009)
Infinite Difference (as editor, Shearsman 2010)
Divining for Starters (Shearsman 2011)

Amy Evans
Dear World & Everyone In It: new poetry in the UK,
    ed. Nathan Hamilton (Bloodaxe 2012).
'Malady' in *Women's Studies Quarterly*, Special Issue
VIRAL, eds. Patricia Clough and Jasbir Puar, New York, Volume 40, Issues
    1 & 2, (Spring/Summer 2012).
'Stalking Gerald Manley Hopkins', 'Arranged Marriage', 'A Language' and
    'The Writer's Portrait' in *Shearsman*, 87 & 88 (April 2011).

Ivano Fermini
Italian Poetry 1950 to 1990 (Dante University Press 1996)
(Ian Seed plans to translate and make available more of Fermini's poetry in
    the near future).

Alec Finlay
Mesostic Remedy (with Linda France & illustrations by Laurie Clark)
    (morning star 2009)
Question your teaspoons (Calder Wood Press 2012)
Be My Reader (Shearsman 2012)

Allen Fisher
Confidence in Lack, essays (Writers Forum 2007)
LEANS (Salt 2007)
PROPOSALS (Spanner 2010)

S.J. Fowler
Red Museum (Knives Forks & Spoons 2011)
Fights: cycle I-XV (Veer 2011)
Minimum Security Prison Dentistry (Anything Anymore Anywhere 2011)

Giles Goodland
What the Things Sang (Shearsman 2009)
Gloss (Knives Forks & Spoons 2011)
Dumb Messengers (Salt 2012)

Catherine Hales
hazard or fall (Shearsman 2010)
Berlin Fresco – Selected Poems of Norbert Hummelt, translated
 and introduced by Catherine Hales (Shearsman 2010)
Infinite Difference (ed. Carrie Etter, Shearsman 2010)

John Hall
Else Here: Selected Poems (Etruscan Books 1999)
Couldn't You? (Shearsman 2007)
Interscriptions (with Peter Hughes) (Knives Forks & Spoons 2011)

Michael Haslam
The Music Laid Her Songs In Language (Arc 2001)
Mid Life (Shearsman 2007)
A Cure for Woodness (Arc 2010)

Ralph Hawkins
Tell Me No More and Tell Me (Grosseteste 19801)
The MOON, the Chief Hairdresser (Highlights) (Shearsman 2004)
Gone to Marzipan (Shearsman 2009)

Peter Hughes
Blue Roads (Salt 2003)
The Summer of Agios Dimitrios (Shearsman 2009)
The Pistol Tree Poems (with Simon Marsh) (Shearsman 2011)

John James
In One Side & Out the Other (with Andrew Crozier and Tom Phillips)
 (Ferry 1970)
Collected Poems (Salt 2002)
In Romsey Town (Equipage 2011)

David Kennedy
The Devil's Bookshop (Salt 2007)
MY Atrocity (Oystercatcher 2009)
Mistral (Rack 2010)

Rachel Lehrman
Second Waking (Oystercatcher 2010)

Gerry Loose
Printed on Water – New & Selected Poems (Shearsman 2007)
From Kyoto to Carbeth (Collins Gallery/Scottish Poetry Library 2008)
that person himself (Shearsman 2009)

Simon Marsh
Bar Magenta (with Peter Hughes) (Many Press 1988)
The Ice Glossaries (Poetical Histories 1997)
The Pistol Tree Poems (with Peter Hughes) (Shearsman 2011)

Sophie Mayer
Her Various Scalpels (Shearsman 2009)
Infinite Difference (ed. Carrie Etter, Shearsman 2010)
Private Parts of Girls (Salt 2011)

Anne Mendelssohn
Bernache nonnette (Equipage 1995)
Implacable Art (Salt 2000)
Py (Oystercatcher 2009)

Richard Moorhead
The Reluctant Vegetarian (Oystercatcher 2009)
Not Only the Dark (World Aid 2011)
Adventures in Form (Penned in the Margins 2012)

Alistair Noon
Some Questions on the Cultural Revolution (Gratton Street Irregulars 2010)
Swamp Area (Longbarrow 2012)
Earth Records (Nine Arches 2012)

Alasdair Paterson
on the governing of empires (Shearsman 2010)
Brumaire and Later (Flarestack 2011)
in arcadia (Oystercatcher 2011)

Simon Perril
Hearing is Itself Suddenly a Kind of Singing (Salt 2004)
A Clutch of Odes (Oystercatcher 2009)
Nitrate (Salt 2010)

Rufo Quintavalle
Make Nothing Happen (Oystercatcher 2009)
Liquiddity (Oystercatcher 2011)
Dog, cock, ape and viper (Corrupt 2011)

Peter Riley
Passing Measures (Carcanet 2003)
The Llyn Writings (Shearsman 2007)

Greek Passages (Shearsman 2009)
The Glacial Stairway (Carcanet 2011)

Sophie Robinson
a (Les Figues 2009)
The Lotion (Oystercatcher 2010)
Infinite Difference (ed. Carrie Etter, Shearsman 2010)

David Rushmer
Homage to Throbbing Gristle (Writers Forum 1992)
The Family of Ghosts (Arehouse 2005)
Blanchot's Ghost (Oystercatcher 2008)

Lisa Samuels
Tomorrowland (Shearsman 2009)
Mama Mortality Corridos (Holloway 2010)
Gender City (Shearsman 2011)
Wild Dialectics (Shearsman 2012)

Maurice Scully
livelihood (Wild Honey 2004)
Doing the Same in English (Dedalus 2008)
Humming (Shearsman 2009)
A Tour of the Lattice (Veer 2011)

Pete Smith
20/20 Vision (Wild Honey 1998)
cross of green hollow (Wild Honey 2001)
Strum of Unseen (above/ground Ottawa 2008)

Matina Stamatakis
Metempsychose (http://ypolitapress.blogspot.com/2009/02/
    metempsychose-by-matina-stamatakis.html)
ek-ae: a Journey into ekphrastic poetics (http://dusie.org/EKAE.pdf)
Xenomorphia (www.wheelhousemagazine.com/chapbook/stamatakis_
    williams.pdf)

Philip Terry
Raymond Queneau, Elementary Morality, (translator)(Carcanet 2007)
Oulipoems 2 (Ahadada 2009)
Shakespeare's Sonnets (Carcanet 2010)

Nathan Thompson
A Haunting (Gratton Street Irregulars 2010)
The Day Maybe Died… Imagining China (Knives Forks & Spoons 2011)
The Visitor's Guest (Shearsman 2011)

Carol Watts
Wrack (Reality Street 2007)
Occasionals (Reality Street 2011)
Sundog (Veer 2012)

John Welch
Collected Poems (Shearsman 2008)
Visiting Exile (Shearsman 2009)
Its Halting Measure (Shearsman 2012)

Nigel Wheale
Raw Skies (Shearsman 2006)
The Six Strides of Freyfaxi (Oystercatcher 2010)
readings at www.archiveofthenow.com